Cities through Time

Daily Life in Ancient and Modern

by Joan D. Barghusen

illustrations by Bob Moulder

R P

Runestone Press/Minneapolis
An imprint of Lerner Publishing Group

The *Cities through Time* series is produced by Runestone Press, an imprint of Lerner Publishing Group, in cooperation with Greenleaf Publishing, Inc., Geneva, Illinois.

Cover design by Michael Tacheny
Text design by Melanie Lawson and Jean DeVaty

Runestone Press
An imprint of Lerner Publishing Group
241 First Avenue North
Minneapolis, Minnesota 55401 U.S.A.

Website address: www.lernerbooks.com

Library of Congress Cataloging-in-Publication Data

Barghusen, Joan D., 1935–
    Daily life in ancient and modern Cairo / by Joan D. Barghusen;
  illustrated by Bob Moulder.
        p. cm. — (Cities through time)
    Includes index.
    Summary: explores daily life in the city of Cairo, from the time of its
  earliest settlement around 3000 B.C. through the Dynasty of Saladin
and the Ottoman Turk rule up to modern times.
    ISBN 0–8225–3221–2 (lib. bdg. : alk. paper)
    1. Cairo (Egypt)—Social life and customs—Juvenile literature.
  2. Cairo (Egypt)—Social conditions—Juvenile literature. 3. Cairo
  (Egypt)—History—Juvenile literature. [1. Cairo (Egypt)] I. Webb, Ray.
  II. Title. III. Series.
    DT146.B37 2001
    962'.16—dc21   99–047839

Manufactured in the United States of America
1 2 3 4 5 6 – JR – 06 05 04 03 02 01

Contents

The view from Cairo's Citadel *(above)* offers a panorama of the city. Standing before the pyramid of King Khafre, the Sphinx *(left)* was built to glorify Egyptian kings.

Introduction

The city of Cairo lies in Egypt at the tip of the Nile Delta. The Nile River branches out here from a single channel and eventually empties into the Mediterranean Sea. Egypt's rulers have long built capitals and fortresses in this area.

The earliest city at the site of modern-day Cairo was Memphis, a capital of ancient Egypt. Beginning in the 2600s B.C., Egyptian pharaohs (kings) built magnificent pyramids and monuments in and around Memphis. They used seasonal workers to build when the waters of the Nile were low. In the 500s B.C., invading Persians built Babylon-in-Egypt across the Nile, a little north of Memphis. Over the centuries to come, this city passed through the hands of the Greeks, the Romans, and the Byzantine Empire.

The town of al-Fustat was founded south of modern Cairo in the A.D. 600s by the first Arabs to conquer Egypt. In 969 the Fatimids, a powerful Muslim family from North Africa, founded the city of al-Qahira (Cairo) at the head of the Nile Delta. Under Fatimid (and later Mamluk) rule, the city became a center of trade and intellectual life in medieval times. After the nearby Ottoman Empire conquered Egypt in the 1500s, Cairo entered a period of decline. Nevertheless, Cairo continued to attract visitors from all over the world. When Europeans took over Egypt in the late 1700s, tourists flocked to see the pharaohs' ancient monuments, still preserved by the dry desert climate.

Modern Cairo is the capital of the Arab Republic of Egypt. More than one thousand years old, the present city straddles both banks of the Nile. Home to more than 13 million residents, Cairo is heir to the diverse traditions of more than five thousand years of Egyptian history.

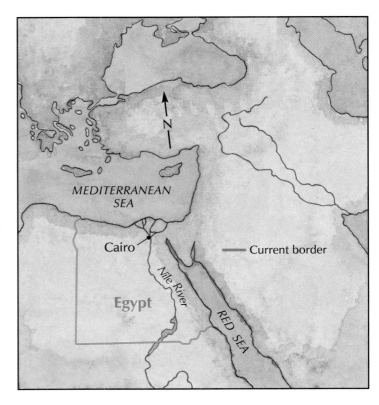

5

Pharaohs and Pyramids

Around 3000 B.C., the first pharaoh united Upper and Lower Egypt into the Kingdom of the Two Lands. He established his capital city of Memphis on the Nile's west bank, at the tip of the delta. From this strategic position, leaders could control and defend both sections of the country.

Egypt's pharaohs lived at Memphis throughout the Old Kingdom—an era that lasted from 2686 to 2181 B.C. Many of Egypt's famous ancient monuments were built during this time. On the outskirts of Memphis, many cemeteries were created with ornate tombs for noble men and women. Pyramids honored pharaohs and their queens. Kings of the Fourth Dynasty, which lasted from 2613 to 2494 B.C., built their pyramids on the nearby Giza Plateau.

Tens of thousands of workers labored for decades to construct the Great Pyramid of Khufu (Cheops), the smaller pyramids of Giza, and the Sphinx. The pyramid builders were peasants, who made up about 80 percent of Egypt's population. Most peasants were farmers. For three months each year, the Nile flooded, making it impossible to farm the riverbanks. So pharaohs forced peasants to quarry, mine, and construct tombs and monuments. At any time, the pharaoh also could demand work for special projects.

Bakers, brewers, potters, brick makers, weavers, launderers, and other laborers provided everyday items and services to the residents of Memphis. The city was also home to sculptors, artists, and painters, who decorated palaces, temples, and tombs. Goldsmiths, coppersmiths, and carpenters manufactured luxury products.

Later pharaohs made the southern city of Thebes their main residence. But Memphis remained one of Egypt's most important cities, linking the Nile Valley with the Mediterranean world. Not until foreigners began to dominate Egypt around 500 B.C. would Memphis begin to decline.

The Sphinx was carved out of an enormous rock left behind by earlier stone quarriers.

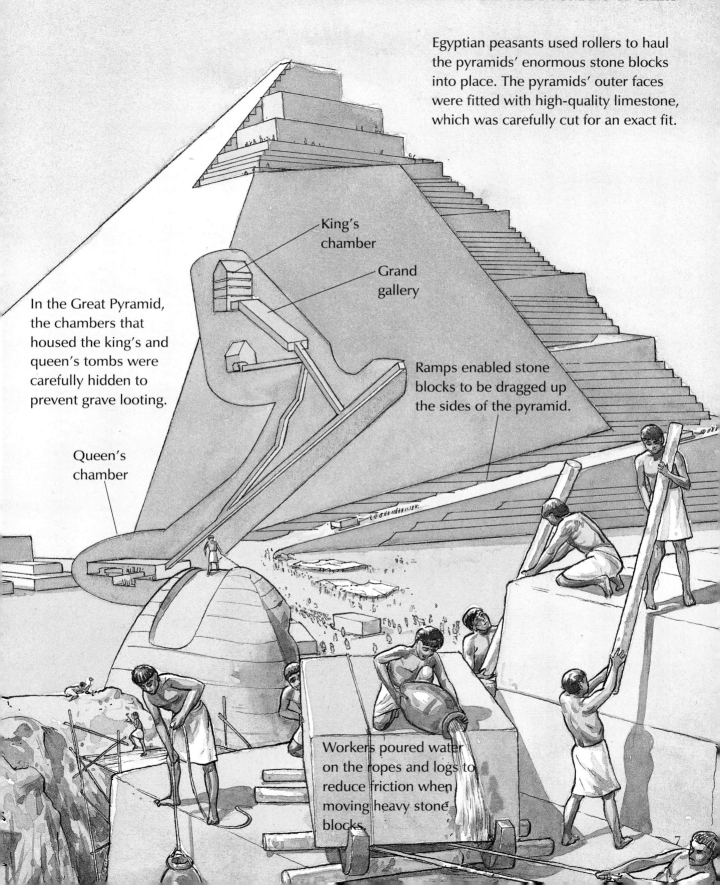

Egyptian peasants used rollers to haul the pyramids' enormous stone blocks into place. The pyramids' outer faces were fitted with high-quality limestone, which was carefully cut for an exact fit.

King's chamber

Grand gallery

In the Great Pyramid, the chambers that housed the king's and queen's tombs were carefully hidden to prevent grave looting.

Ramps enabled stone blocks to be dragged up the sides of the pyramid.

Queen's chamber

Workers poured water on the ropes and logs to reduce friction when moving heavy stone blocks.

7

Babylon-in-Egypt

In 525 B.C., the Persian Empire took control of Egypt. At the site called Babylon-in-Egypt, across the Nile just north of Memphis, the Persians opened a canal as part of a long waterway. The canal connected the Nile with the nearby Red Sea so that Egyptian grain and other products could be shipped east to Persia.

In 332 B.C., the Macedonian general Alexander the Great and his Greek army conquered Egypt. Alexander visited Memphis before establishing Alexandria, far to the north. Greek became the official language of Cairo, and the old Egyptian hieroglyphic (picture) writing died out. The Greek alphabet was used to write the native Egyptian language, which came to be known as *Coptic.* This word comes from *Aegyptos,* the Greek name for Egypt. Greeks and Egyptians lived side by side, and some intermarried. Citizens worshiped Greek gods along with traditional Egyptian deities, especially the goddess Isis. Artisans made highly prized textiles decorated with lively human figures, animals, and plant forms.

In 30 B.C., the Roman Empire took over Egypt. Romans built a fort at Babylon-in-Egypt. Locals provided goods and services to the Roman soldiers there. Soon the new religion of Christianity spread to Egypt, and most Egyptians adopted the faith. Egyptian Christians became known as Copts. The Copts built several churches in Babylon-in-Egypt, decorating them with crosses, saints, and biblical scenes.

In A.D. 395, the Roman Empire split in two. The eastern half, which included Babylon-in-Egypt, became part of the Byzantine Empire. When Arab conquerors reached the town in 640, they found a settlement of Coptic Christians nestled alongside the old fortress walls. The remains of Babylon-in-Egypt would eventually become part of Old Cairo. With its ancient Coptic churches still standing, this area remains an important center for Cairo's Christian population.

Coptic grave carvings *(inset)* often contained religious images. Experts believe the remains of a fresco of four of Jesus' apostles *(right)* are from an ancient Coptic church.

All types of porcelain are made at al-Fustat. It is so fine and transparent that a hand held outside a vase can be seen through it. Bowls, cups, dishes, and other utensils are made here.

—Nasir-i Khusraw,
a Persian visitor to Cairo

A City of Tents

The Arab army that entered Babylon-in-Egypt in 640 drove out the inhabitants and set up camp outside the city's northern walls. This tent city was called al-Fustat. Many Arab soldiers brought along their wives and children, who settled in al-Fustat. The Arab army also brought the Arabic language and the Islamic religion, founded by the prophet Muhammad only fifty years earlier.

Followers of Islam are called Muslims. Muslims are divided into two branches: Sunni and Shia. They differ over the leadership of Islam, but all Muslims are united by their faith in Allah (God). Muslims pray five times a day and fast during the holy month of Ramadan. All Muslim men are expected to attend public prayers each Friday in the town mosques (places of worship). Women are not permitted inside most mosques, although some have special areas for women.

Under Arab rule, many Egyptians adopted the Islamic religion. But others remained Christians. Along with Copts, Jews, and all other non-Muslims, they were forced to pay a special tax. Arab newcomers relied on the local residents for food and manufactured goods. Egyptians worked as accountants and clerks, keeping records in Coptic or Greek. Egyptian architects and artisans built stone and mud-brick structures.

Over the years, al-Fustat and Babylon-in-Egypt became one city. Tall buildings—some with 14 stories housing 200 people—replaced earlier structures. Local workers manufactured glassware, ceramics, and other products for trade. The city was a lively commercial port, and travelers praised its markets.

Two new Islamic dynasties (series of rulers from one family)—the Abbasids and the Tulunids—later conquered Egypt. They built the grand palace cities of Medinat al-Askar and al-Qatai in the area. But these cities were eventually abandoned when their rulers lost power. Al-Fustat, however, remained an important center of city life and commerce.

Cairo Is Founded

By 969 the Fatimids, a North African family who claimed direct descent from the prophet Muhammad, had conquered Egypt. Unlike the Sunni Muslims already in Egypt, the Fatimids were Shia Muslims, or Shiites. Besides ruling Egypt, the Fatimids controlled Syria and western Arabia, which claimed the Islamic holy cities of Mecca and Medina.

The new Fatimid ruler founded his royal city, al-Qahira, or Cairo, on open land a few miles north of al-Fustat. Cairo was carefully planned and laid out with palaces for the ruler, his family, and other members of the court. Running between the west and east palaces was the main north-south street of the city. Markets lined the street from the city's northern gate, Bab al-Futuh, to its southern gate, Bab Zuwayla. The first mosque in Cairo, al-Azhar, was completed in 971. Near the ruler's palace, it was large enough to hold all the royal residents and military troops of the city.

Soldiers lived in the city and just outside its walls. The unruly troops often fought with each other. So they were housed in different sections according to their ethnic origin—Greek, Armenian, Sudanese, and Turkish, to name a few. This separation reduced ethnic tension and brawling among the ranks.

Al-Fustat continued to be the center of commercial and day-to-day Egyptian life. Cairo, on the other hand, was a seat of royalty, military power, and enormous wealth. Visitors to the city reported seeing sacks of precious jewels, crystal vases, beautiful gardens with fountains, and a thousand palace guards.

On ceremonial occasions—such as the yearly Plenitude of the Nile festival to celebrate the river's rising—the people of Cairo and al-Fustat came together. Then the sultan (ruler) appeared in a parade. He threw coins to the cheering crowd and provided a feast for everyone.

Fatimid warriors clash with enemy forces in this twelfth-century mural *(above)*. Skillful fighters, the Fatimids also spent much time carefully planning the construction of Cairo. Close to the Nile River, the city had plenty of water to irrigate crops and fish and other wildlife for food.

The bride is completely veiled.

Marriage and Family

Most of Cairo's young men and women married. Their parents or other family members arranged the marriages. In many cases, the bride and groom would not even meet until the wedding. Girls married young, usually by the age of sixteen. Boys were often older—they needed to establish careers so they could support a family. While men were allowed to have as many as four wives, most could afford only one. The groom paid a dowry, or marriage gift,

to the bride's family. According to *sharia* (Islamic law), the wife would receive one-third of this gift when her husband died or if he divorced her.

The marriage ceremony itself consisted of a few sentences and the joining of hands. But celebrations with feasting and dancing sometimes lasted for days. A procession accompanied the bride to her new home in the groom's household.

Married couples wanted children. It was considered a great misfortune for a

At the groom's house, the family waits expectantly to welcome the new bride.

family to be childless. Having children brought a wife status and made it unlikely that her husband would divorce her. Divorce was a simple matter for men, who had only to state the end of the marriage in front of witnesses. But if a woman wanted a divorce against her husband's wishes, she had to take her case before the *qadi*, or Islamic judge. The judge heard cases at or near the mosque. Court records show that sometimes women were granted divorces, especially when witnesses testified that the husband had mistreated his wife.

Children often died from sickness. Even a woman who gave birth to many sons and daughters might raise only a few to adulthood. Children were expected to be obedient and respectful toward their parents—especially to their father. His authority over the family was unquestioned. Girls remained at home until their marriage. Around the age of seven, a boy might go to school. By the age of twelve or so, he was likely to be working as an apprentice and learning his father's trade.

At Home

A family of comfortable means lived in a two- or three-storied, flat-roofed house of stone and brick. Rooms were arranged around a courtyard for privacy from the noisy, crowded street. In richer households, the courtyard might have a well or fountain.

On the first floor were stables, servants' rooms, a kitchen, and a small reception room for visitors. Male guests were entertained in an open-air sitting room on the second floor or in a large, high-ceilinged room also used as a family sitting room.

On the upper floors, private rooms were set aside for female family members. These quarters were called the harem, a word that referred both to the space and to the women who lived in it. Windows in the harem had latticed wooden shutters to let in air and light while protecting privacy. From behind the shutters, women watched activities in the street or courtyard below.

Only men who were family members or close relatives entered the harem. The harem was a sign of high social status. People at lower social levels imitated the system as much as possible. But poor families often lived in one- or two-room apartments in large buildings. Their small quarters had no room for a harem.

At all economic levels, people had little furniture. They sat on built-in window seats or lay on raised platforms covered with mats and cushions. At night the family brought mattresses out of cupboards. Families ate meals at small, movable tables. Kitchens were simple, and many Cairenes (citizens of Cairo) bought prepared food from market shops. People ate their meals quickly but lingered over coffee or tea.

The harem

Men's sitting room

Kitchen

Courtyard

Servants' quarters

Stables

17

Egyptians near Cairo bring livestock to drink along the banks of the Nile River.

Life on the Nile

Most of Cairo depended on the Nile River for its water. The city was situated away from the river, beyond the reach of flooding. So a canal, forming Cairo's western boundary, brought the river's water to the city. From this Cairo Canal, men used donkeys to transport water to Cairo for drinking and household use. Thousands of water carriers, their waterbags flung over their backs, walked the streets, stopping to sell a drink or fill a merchant's earthenware container.

Aqueducts (elevated canals) sometimes carried water to the palaces, and some wealthy homes had their own wells. But most people went to bathhouses, and many obtained household water from public fountains. Wealthy people often constructed these as an act of charity.

On the low-lying ground between the canal and the river, floodwaters created

The day of plenitude came, which was Rajab 16 [August 7], and the Sultan embarked at the Kharrubiya and proceeded to the Nilometer with the emirs [nobles] and government officials. He perfumed the Nilometer according to custom, then sailed into the Cairo Canal to the dam, which he opened.

—Ibn Taghribirdi,
a fifteenth-century Muslim historian

ponds—including Lake Ezbekiya, a popular recreation spot. Farmers used the river and its ponds and canals to irrigate the grain fields, vegetable plots, and orchards that fed Cairo. These waters also provided fish, which people netted and sold in the city markets.

A device called the Nilometer on the island of Roda, opposite al-Fustat, measured the river's annual rise. When the floodwaters had reached the desired level, the city rejoiced. At a signal from the sultan, an earthen dam was broken to release the river's flow into the Cairo Canal. Families gathered along the shore and boarded torchlit barges on the water, singing and feasting to celebrate the Plenitude of the Nile festival.

Over time, the natural shifting of the river's current caused the Nile to gradually move toward the west. As the riverbanks moved west, the land between the Nile and the Cairo Canal became drier. As Cairo grew, residents settled west of the canal. By 1400 the canal ran through the middle of the expanded city.

In the rooms of this palace were placed beds, fully appointed, for lying patients. At the disposal of the intendant are servants whose duty it is, morning and evening, to examine the conditions of the sick, and to bring them the food and potions that befit them. Facing this establishment is another specially for women, and they also have persons to attend them.

—Moorish traveler Ibn Juybar, visiting Saladin's hospital soon after it was established

Cairo under Saladin

By 1168 the Fatimids had lost control of Syria. Crusaders—Christian European soldiers fighting a series of religious wars called the Crusades—controlled Jerusalem and the rest of the Holy Land. They threatened to take over Cairo as well.

Walls protected the city but not the nearby town of al-Fustat. Fearing the Crusaders would seize al-Fustat to weaken Cairo, Fatimid leaders set fire to the town. Al-Fustat burned for more than fifty days, and its people fled into Cairo.

An army from Damascus, Syria, saved Cairo from the Crusaders. Saladin, a general in the Syrian army, became the new sultan of Egypt. Under his rule, Egypt returned to Sunni Islam.

Saladin made other important changes in Cairo. He ordered Crusaders who had been captured as prisoners of war to help build a new fortress called the Citadel. The laborers used stones from small pyramids to build the fortress and its surrounding walls. Saladin and his troops lived at the Citadel, which stood high in the rocky Mokattam Hills. Overlooking southeastern Cairo, the Citadel became a center of military power.

Saladin's Cairo, several times as large as the original Cairo, was no longer just a royal city or a city of soldiers. It was a home for common people as well. They built their homes around the old palaces, city gates, mosques, and the Citadel itself. The neatly laid out Fatimid city disappeared, covered by an unplanned tangle of streets, shops, and houses.

Saladin built many *madrasas*, or religious schools, to educate Cairenes about Islam. And the *maristan*, or hospital, he set up became famous as a model of medical practice.

When the Syrian general Saladin *(above)* became sultan of Egypt, he extended the city walls *(left)* to include the remains of al-Fustat, or Old Cairo, to the south and to the Nile River on the north.

The Warrior Class

The Mamluks of Cairo were Muslim slave-soldiers, most often Turkish or Circassian—from an area north of Turkey, between the northwestern Caucasus Mountains and the northeastern coast of the Black Sea. Slave dealers captured or purchased them as young boys, converted them to Islam, and sent them to training camps. After a Mamluk's training was complete, he was freed, but he still owed military service to his former owner.

In 1250 the Mamluks began a rise to rulership. They were aided by a very unusual event—the rule of a woman. Shajrat al-Durr was a Turkish slave married to the sultan of Cairo. When her husband died in the Crusades, Shajrat al-Durr—supported by the Mamluks—took control of the government. But the caliph of Baghdad, who was the spiritual head of Sunni Islam, refused to accept a woman as a Muslim leader. He threatened to send a ruler of his own choice. To keep her power, the queen married one of the Mamluks. But when her new husband planned to take a second wife, Shajrat al-Durr had him murdered. Rising against the queen, the Mamluks in turn had her killed. They chose a new Mamluk as sultan, a position that Mamluks would hold for 250 years.

For many years, the Mamluks' military strength protected Egypt, and their reign was prosperous. They enjoyed luxury crafts and built impressive monuments. They continued to bring other Mamluks to Cairo until these slave-soldiers made up a foreign ruling class in the city. Many grew wealthy and established large households, usually marrying women from their homelands. Most Mamluks did not speak Arabic, as did the native Egyptians. The warrior rulers remained separate from the common people in everything but religion.

> *There are twelve Mamluk barracks, each one of which is almost as long as a street and can hold up to a thousand Mamluks. The interior court of the palace is enormous, and in it are a vast garden and a small pond. The stables in which the ruler's horses are kept are also very large and many in number.*
>
> —Description of parts of Cairo's Citadel by the fifteenth-century writer Khalil al-Zahiri

Most of Cairo's slave-soldiers, the Mamluks, lived in and around the city's Citadel, where they kept their horses and practiced their military skills on large, open grounds.

Every neighborhood had its own mosque.

The local sheik maintained order in the neighborhood.

A Mamluk on horseback

Streets were unpaved, and to keep down the dust, people sometimes sprinkled them with water.

24

Neighborhood Life

Building awnings helped protect pedestrians from the blazing sun.

In the Middle Ages (roughly between A.D. 500 and 1500), only a few of Cairo's streets led through the city from end to end. Most streets were short. The residential districts of the city were a maze of alleys and lanes. The medieval writer al-Maqrizi reported in the early 1400s that Cairo had 37 *harat*, or quarters.

Each of these quarters was a *hara*, or neighborhood. A main street entered the hara and branched out into many smaller dead-end streets and alleys. At night a gate or chain across the main street closed off the neighborhood from the rest of the city, and a doorkeeper guarded the entrance. The typical quarter had a small mosque, its own markets and coffee shops, and perhaps a community fountain. These neighborhoods often formed around people connected by ethnic background, religion, or occupation. The dwellings of rich and poor often stood side by side. Many poor people clustered around wealthier households that employed them for services. Within each quarter, a *sheik* (chief) was responsible for keeping order and collecting taxes.

Cairo's streets were narrow, sometimes less than three feet wide. Travelers on foot dodged loaded camels and donkeys, and everyone yielded to Mamluks on horseback. Although crowded, the streets offered one great advantage in Cairo's hot climate—shade. The shadows cast by connected buildings shielded the streets from the blazing sun. Awnings and mats stretched between buildings for more protection.

Property owners along a street were responsible for its upkeep. Since there were no building regulations, an owner might set up a shop, install a stone *mastaba* (bench) in front of the shop, or even enlarge a house onto the public way. Over time, Cairo's narrow streets grew even more crowded,

The World of Women

A woman in Cairo during the medieval period typically lived with her parents until marriage. Then she lived in her husband's home, subject to the control of her mother-in-law or other older female members of her husband's family. She was expected to bear children and to behave modestly and honorably. Her place was in the home, where her family and children respected her.

While wealthy women spent most of their time at home, they were not always confined to the harem. They went out on foot or rode donkeys to visit relatives, public baths, or the tombs of saints. When in public, they were required to wear a veil and to be escorted by male servants or family members. At home, wealthy women occupied themselves with needlework, entertaining relatives, and buying wares from door-to-door tradeswomen.

Tradeswomen and other less wealthy women were often unveiled. They moved about on the streets more freely in the course of their day's activities. But most

likely they stayed within their own neighborhoods.

Few women in Cairo knew how to read. Those who were educated taught other women to read and write, and even became highly respected as holy women. Women also worked as healers and midwives (people who assist during childbirth).

While women seldom had public power, they were important members of the networks formed by marriage and family connections. It was not uncommon for a woman to manage wealth—either a portion of the family finances or her own property. Some women rented out houses or shops and ran businesses. And many wealthy women gave money to charitable and religious institutions.

Most of Cairo's wealthy women lived in harems inside their households. Servants and slaves helped them dress, served them meals *(left)*, and helped care for their children. Women only visited with men who were close relatives. And when women were sick, they received care from holy men and doctors *(above)*.

Educating the Young

When a child was born in medieval Cairo, its father recited the call to prayer in his or her right ear. This ritual was thought to protect the infant from evil. If the baby was a boy, the father chose his name. If the baby was a girl, the mother named her. Parents swaddled, or tightly wrapped, the newborn, which they believed was necessary to protect its weak arms and legs.

Mothers cared for the children, often with the help of servants or slave girls. By the age of two, babies were weaned and ate the same food as the family. Dolls, toy animals, and balls were among their favorite toys. If the household had a harem, young boys stayed there with their mothers until the age of seven. It was a mark of respect for children to greet their father by kissing his hand.

The lives of girls centered on the home, as would their lives as women. They learned the skills and tasks of household management that would be their responsibility as adults. Sometimes they learned needlework, especially embroidery, from a special teacher.

At the age of six or seven, most boys went to school. Almost every mosque had a school where boys learned to read the Koran, the sacred scriptures of Islam. Students also studied beginning writing and simple arithmetic. The memorization required for lessons was often boring, and many teachers beat students to make them learn.

By the time they were around twelve, boys who were entering trades left school to begin their professional training. Further education was only for scholars or physicians. Large mosques, such as al-Azhar, had madrasas, or religious schools, where scholars taught advanced subjects of the Islamic religion.

> *Prevention of the child from playing games and constant insistence on learning deadens his heart, blunts his sharpness of wit and burdens his life; he looks for a ruse to escape [his studies] altogether.*
>
> —Advice of eleventh-century theologian al-Ghazali to parents and teachers

Male pupils could continue their education and improve their status in society by becoming teachers or religious scholars. Although boys and girls are shown in a classroom together *(right)*, coeducation was uncommon in medieval Cairo.

All classes of the population, both men and women, assemble for this ceremony, then they go in procession with the mahmil round the two cities of Cairo and al-Fustat, accompanied by all those whom we have mentioned, and with the camel drivers singing to their camels in the lead....

—Description of the mahmil festival by Ibn Battuta, a fourteenth-century visitor to Cairo

Mamluks parade through the streets.

Singers and dancers, accompanied by musicians, entertain the crowds.

Holiday Celebrations

People from all walks of life, rich and poor, came together for Cairo's great religious celebrations. The most important was Ramadan, a month-long period of fasting. During Ramadan, Muslims take no food or drink during daylight hours, and the pace of life quiets. With darkness, the city came alive. Families gathered to eat and enjoy public entertainments. People celebrated the end of Ramadan with a great feast of rejoicing. This was also the time for paying *zakat*, the contribution Muslims are required to make to charity.

One of Cairo's most spectacular events was the Mawlid al-Nabi, a celebration in honor of the prophet Muhammad's birthday. This was a huge fair that drew people from remote areas. Festivities began the night before with a torchlight procession from the Citadel. On the day itself, important officials gave speeches, and the Mamluks paraded on their exercise grounds.

Feasting and entertainment was provided by wealthy members of the elite for everyone. Tables of food were set out on the parade grounds. Singers, dancers, snake charmers, puppet shows, and storytellers amused the crowds of men, women, and children.

Another colorful holiday occurred when the *mahmil*—an elegant wooden structure—was mounted on a fine, tall camel and led through the city. Richly decorated with gold and embroidered cloths, the mahmil carried a Koran. Crowds of people turned out to see this parade with its escort of holy men and Mamluks in colorful outfits. Then the mahmil accompanied the annual pilgrimage caravan to Mecca. Islamic law requires every Muslim to make at least one such trip in his or her lifetime.

Smaller local events also provided occasions for celebrating. Weddings and funerals often included public processions, with food offered to any and all who came. At these events, the wealthy shared their food with the poor, an act of kindness that brought blessings to the giver as well as the receiver.

A snake charmer amazes an audience of children.

31

*I find the baker's kindness far
  from negligible,
Since I buy from him on credit,
And he ignores my failure to
  pay.*
  —Words from a popular song
    of the fifteenth century

Shoppers in Cairo's crowded marketplace were guaranteed a fair price, since merchants selling similar items occupied stalls next to each other. Even so, shoppers and vendors alike enjoyed the art of bargaining.

Artisans and Tradespeople

Cairo was filled with artisans, craftspeople, and tradespeople. They furnished the city's everyday needs, from bread and cooked foods to needles and shoes. They also produced its luxuries, such as gold bracelets and perfumes. Often people sold goods from the same small workshop in which they produced the items.

Workers and shops of a particular trade were usually located on the same street or in the same market. Grain merchants, slave dealers, needle makers, leather workers, food sellers, dyers, embroiderers, and many other businesses each had a special area. Most were located along Cairo's main north-south street. The street of the sword makers, however, was closer to the Citadel for the convenience of its Mamluk customers.

A large market of copper and brass workers was situated in the main market area of the city. The Mamluks, who prized the beautifully decorated objects, encouraged these highly skilled workers. Artisans made bowls, trays, candlesticks, pen cases, and other objects for use in the household or mosque. Some designs were imprinted with the name of the man or woman for whom the item was made. Large brass or copper trays from this market were popular in homes that could afford them.

Shops themselves were tiny, only about six feet square. They opened onto the street on the ground level of a larger building, and they sometimes had another room at the back for storage. At the front, the shopkeeper sat on a bench with customers to drink tea or coffee and negotiate prices.

A market inspector, who was in charge of regulating weights and measures, supervised market activities. He also collected taxes and was responsible for seeing that business practices were fair and reasonable. Each trade or craft had its own sheik who approved new members, settled disputes, and helped the market inspector with taxes.

33

It is said, O wise and happy King, that once there was a prosperous merchant who had abundant wealth and investments and commitments in every country. He had many women and children and kept many servants and slaves.

—"Story of the Merchant and the Demon" from *One Thousand and One Nights*

Merchants and Caravans

Some of Cairo's richest residents were long-distance merchants. These businesspeople, or their agents, brought products from many countries into Egypt by boat and by camel caravan. Slaves and luxury products came from farther south in Africa, spices from India and Southeast Asia, and silks from China.

Until 1500, when Europeans discovered they could sail to India by going around Africa, Egypt's merchants monopolized trade with Southeast Asia. Wealthy spice traders bought pepper and other spices in India and sold them, at enormous profits, in the markets of Cairo. Some of the spices were shipped to European markets, where they brought even higher prices. Since the government heavily taxed this long-distance trade, it was the source of much of medieval Cairo's wealth. Cairene merchants and shopkeepers are featured in the famous collection of stories called *One Thousand and One Nights*. Told and retold by storytellers, these folk tales were first written down in Cairo.

Merchants brought Southeast Asian products by boat as far as Suez, near the north end of the Red Sea. The old canal that had linked the Red Sea to the Nile near the port at al-Fustat was no longer in use. So merchants loaded their goods onto camels for the last leg of the trip across the desert to Cairo. Around 1400 a new port called Bulaq was built north of al-Fustat. The new port was more conveniently located to receive the overland caravans with their valuable merchandise.

At Bulaq, merchants found large inns called *khans*, where they could rest at the end of their long journeys. Besides offering rooms for the merchants, khans provided stables for camels and donkeys, safe storage spaces for wares, and a place to conduct business. Some wealthy Cairene merchants and Mamluks founded their own khans. One was the Khan el-Khalili, established by the man in charge of the sultan's horses. Located in the center of the old Fatimid city, the Khan el-Khalili is still at the heart of Cairo's most famous tourist market and is still known by that name.

Traveling camel caravans *(top left)* supplied Cairo's merchants and shoppers *(bottom left)* with a variety of goods. Caravan merchants worked hard, battling the harsh desert climate and occasional attacks by bandits.

A Center of Learning

Medieval Cairo attracted scholars from all over the Islamic world. They came to teach and to learn, and they added their own cultures and knowledge to the city's traditions. Cairo had many schools and libraries where scholars pursued science, history, and religious studies. The university at the al-Azhar Mosque became the foremost school of Islamic studies. There, sheiks taught theology, sharia, arithmetic, logic, and classical Arabic language and literature. These courses prepared students to interpret the law and to compose letters and documents—skills they would need to serve as qadis and as other officials.

Al-Azhar's students were divided into groups that studied with particular learned men. Each sheik taught in a certain part of the mosque. Students lived at the mosque, in quarters divided according to the area from which they came. Cooks prepared their meals in the mosque kitchen, and students often received gifts of clothing, books, paper, and pens. These came from endowments—contributions of money that wealthy people gave to the mosque.

Because Islamic scholars shared a knowledge of the Arabic language, many of them traveled widely, studying and visiting mosques, holy men, and Sufi retreats. People from all walks of life revered Sufi sheiks, some of whom were women. Sufis sought a direct knowledge of God and worshiped in nontraditional ways that included chanting and dancing.

Muslim scholars from all over the world flocked to the university at the al-Azhar Mosque (*right*), which was the foremost school of Islamic studies in Cairo.

*Traveling in pursuit of knowledge
and for the purpose of meeting new
teachers makes learning more
perfect.*

—Scholar Ibn Khaldun

Plague and Famine

During the Middle Ages, periodic epidemics of the plague struck Cairo, causing many deaths. With no effective treatment, the plague was the most feared illness. Victims developed swellings and fever and usually died within five days. The plague spread to humans by fleas from infected rats, which thrived on Cairo's garbage. However, people thought the disease came from bad air, and so they surrounded themselves with flowers and perfumes.

To try to prevent the disease, some people ate certain fruits, and others used magical charms. During outbreaks, officials offered special prayers in the mosques or led processions to pray in the desert.

The "Black Death" plague that swept Europe and the Mediterranean in the fourteenth century devastated Cairo. Almost half the population—about 200,000 people—died in the winter of 1348 and 1349. Many of the dead were Mamluks, slaves, children, and foreigners.

It was established during this epidemic that no infant survived more than a day or two after its birth, and its mother followed it into the grave.
—Fourteenth-century historian al-Maqrizi, describing the plague of 1348

Officials held mass funerals and dug mass graves. But some unburied bodies remained in the streets. Shop owners closed their businesses and abandoned their property. The sultan himself left town.

From 1348 to 1517, the plague returned to Cairo about every five years. The plague was often accompanied by famine (widespread hunger). When large numbers of workers died from the plague, crops were not tended, grain lay in port, and bread was not baked. In addition, if the flooding of the Nile produced either too much or too little water for crops, food supplies were further harmed. Weakened by hunger, people became more vulnerable to disease.

By 1517 plague and famine had dramatically reduced Cairo's population and its wealth. The plague killed thousands more in 1619. And as late as 1835, plague would strike again, killing one-third of the city's people.

[Cairo's walls] *are at present all covered with Ruines, which are so high, that I have passed over some places where they wholly hide the Walls. . . . And though it would be very easie to clear the Rubbish, and by repairing what is wanting, make the Walls appear beautiful and high, yet the Turks make no Reparations, but suffer all to run to decay. . . .*

—Monsieur de Thevenot,
a French visitor to Cairo in 1686

The Ottoman Turks Take Cairo

In 1517 Ottoman Turks attacked Cairo. Women, children, and six thousand slaves helped prepare the city's defenses, but their Mamluk defenders were no match for the Turks with their firearms. Ottoman troops occupied Cairo, killed many Mamluks, and hanged the last Mamluk sultan at Bab Zuwayla, the city's southern gate.

A *pasha*, or Ottoman governor, moved into the Citadel. Slave troops called Janissaries—the most disciplined and skilled units of the Ottoman army—supported the pasha. Unlike the Mamluks, who were horsemen armed with bows and arrows, Janissaries were foot soldiers trained to use the arquebus, a handheld gun.

Educated and trained at the Ottoman emperor's court, each Janissary also learned a trade. Some Janissaries grew wealthy from their businesses, founding great households.

Over time the Mamluks regained their privileged positions. Some became local governors called *beys*. These powerful men controlled lands, businesses, and other sources of wealth.

The Ottoman Empire taxed every enterprise of artisans, tradespeople, merchants, and farmers. The beys collected their own share of this tax money as well as the government's. Beys might order a beating of workers unable to pay. Sometimes the rulers took away the tools of people's trades, leaving them unable to earn a living. Some lands were left untilled as peasants deserted the fields, fleeing to escape punishment for not paying taxes.

Cairo lost its control of the spice trade about the same time the Ottomans arrived. Without the extravagant wealth from the Southeast Asian spice trade, Cairo declined in prosperity.

As the beys, the Mamluks, and other heads of powerful households exploited the workers in Cairo and the countryside, most of the city's residents grew poorer. If they did have wealth, they tried not to show it, for signs of prosperity only attracted the tax collectors.

Some Janissaries worked with Cairo merchants *(top),* offering to protect them in exchange for money. Cairo fell into disrepair under Ottoman rule. Poor people lived in some of the ruined buildings, such as the mosque of Khalif Hakem *(bottom).*

Cairo's Poor

Cairo had a large population of poor people. They performed low-paying jobs looked down on by society. Men worked as day laborers, donkey drivers, garbage collectors, or dog handlers. Women were household servants, singers, or professional mourners at funerals. The poor lived wherever they could. They built hovels in courtyards, against city walls, or among the piles of rubbish in the remains of burned-out al-Fustat. Some moved into and around tombs in the "cities of the dead"—large cemeteries in southern and eastern parts of the city.

The city had many charitable institutions, such as the Mansuri Hospital. It had wards for men and women and a building for the insane. When patients were discharged, they received a small allowance to help them until they could find work.

Some of the poor were beggars who lived on handouts and slept in mosques or on the streets. Others were thieves who operated in gangs that preyed on the city's residents. Some formed an underworld mob. This mob had its own leader. Government officials sometimes asked him to organize the mob to march in parades or to take part in demonstrations. When necessary, the mob did distasteful tasks, such as removing abandoned bodies during plagues. Or they were enlisted to fight during periods of unrest.

Wealthy citizens had, throughout the years, helped care for the needy of Cairo. But when the wealth of Cairo declined, so did the money available for charity. As Egypt's fortune decreased in Ottoman times, the plight of the poor worsened.

Islam requires the wealthy to give money to the poor. So Cairo's poor people *(above)* were able to survive living in streets and cemeteries. Many of the poor gathered in Cairo's South Valley *(facing page)*.

Hard Times

By the late 1700s, Cairo was no longer prosperous. Deserted and neglected structures crumbled into decay, and ruins and rubbish heaps multiplied. At this time, Cairo consisted of the central city, still separated by open lands from the two port areas of al-Fustat (which came to be known as Old Cairo) and Bulaq. People lived and worked, as they had for centuries, in different quarters of the city, depending on their ethnic origin, religion, or occupation.

About 90 percent of Cairo's residents were Muslims. Some were the Arab-Egyptian shopkeepers and artisans who made up the middle class of Cairene society. Most of them lived in the central city, conveniently near markets and commercial streets. But an even larger number of Muslims were peasants or unskilled workers. Many were recent immigrants from rural areas. They found homes in older, deteriorating neighborhoods.

The Turks and Circassians who formed the military and ruling elite were also Muslims. Some still lived in and around the Citadel. Others moved to residential areas such as Ezbekiya, which had palatial homes that overlooked a lake.

Most of Cairo's non-Muslim residents were Coptic Christians, who lived in port areas where they worked as accountants or customs officials. Other religious minorities included Jews, who had lived for centuries in the central area of the city. A few Christian Europeans, mostly wealthy traders, lived in the city's growing European quarter. About 12,000 Nubians and Ethiopians from lands just south of Egypt also lived in the city. They had been brought to Cairo as slaves or unskilled workers.

By the end of the eighteenth century, many of Cairo's buildings were crumbling. To bring in a little income, young boys hawk donkeys for hire *(inset)*. (Both photos were taken in the 1800s, after the invention of photography.)

[Cairo's] *environs are full of heaps of dirt, formed by the rubbish…. Within the walls, the streets are winding and narrow… unpaved.*
—Monsieur Volney, French traveler to Cairo, 1783

Napoleon Takes Cairo

The Ottoman Empire weakened over time, leaving its territories vulnerable to invasion. French general Napoleon Bonaparte marched on Egypt, hoping to make it a province of France. In 1798, after bitter fighting, the French reached Cairo. Cairo's people were terrified and outraged when the French army used the sacred al-Azhar Mosque as a stable for their horses.

Napoleon took for his residence a governor's palace in Ezbekiya. He tried to rule Cairo through the *ulama*—the educated, religious men of the city. Some Cairenes cooperated, but others led revolts against the non-Muslim invaders.

Napoleon himself eventually left Egypt, and the people of Cairo rose up against the remaining French occupiers. When the fighting ended, the port of Bulaq had been looted and burned and much of Ezbekiya destroyed by fire. The French held on to control of the city. They mapped Cairo and planned changes to modernize it.

Engineers trained in Europe worked to improve the city's streets so that the military could move about the city more quickly. French officials ordered the destruction of the gates that separated Cairo's quarters and cleared access to Cairo's northern gates. The route to Ezbekiya, where the French headquarters was located, was widened. And the road from Ezbekiya to the port at Bulaq was shifted above the level to which the Nile usually flooded. These new streets became major thoroughfares of the modern city.

The French takeover was brief. By 1801 a combined British and Ottoman army had driven the French out of Egypt. But Cairo had been opened to European influence, and interest flowed in both directions. While Cairenes did not like French rule, many admired the science and technologies of the Europeans. And Europeans were fascinated by French reports of Egypt, its ancient culture, and the customs of its people.

They plundered whatever they found in the mosque, such as furnishings, vessels, bowls, deposits, and hidden things from closets and cupboards. They treated the books and Koranic volumes as trash, throwing them on the ground, stamping on them with feet and shoes.

—Historian al-Jabarti, describing French treatment of the al-Azhar Mosque

French general Napoleon Bonaparte *(facing page)* and his forces occupied Cairo from 1798 until 1801. Equipped with superior firearms and military training, the French easily put down Egyptian revolts *(above)*.

The female children are very seldom taught to read or write; and not many of them, even among the higher orders, learn to say their prayers....[But] the young daughters of persons of the middle classes are sometimes instructed with the boys in a public school; but they are usually veiled and hold no intercourse with the boys. I have often seen a well-dressed girl reading the Koran in a boys' school.

—Edward William Lane, British visitor to Cairo during the time of Muhammad Ali

Muhammad Ali and Ismail

Egypt was still part of the Ottoman Empire in the 1800s. Cairo's new Ottoman pasha, Muhammad Ali, ruled with little interference from the Ottomans. In 1811 he ended Mamluk power by murdering more than four hundred Mamluk chiefs. A new army of native-born Egyptians, led by Turkish and European officers, supported him.

With unchallenged military strength, Muhammad Ali grew more powerful by taking lands and financial privileges from the wealthy. Ali was eager to adopt European ways. So he sent Egyptian students to France to learn European technologies. He established government schools in Cairo, hiring foreign teachers. He imported French engineers for building projects.

Following Muhammad Ali's example, the rulers who followed him continued to modernize Cairo. They built railways, installed gas lines, and laid pipes to bring water to the city from the Nile. Most of the changes began in the city's European districts. But straight, new roads frequently cut through older neighborhoods. Workers routinely destroyed ancient buildings that stood in the way of construction.

In 1869 the Egyptian pasha Ismail opened the Suez Canal, linking the Mediterranean Sea with the Red Sea. Once again Cairo became a stopping point for travelers and trade between Europe and Asia.

Other changes could be seen by the late 1800s. With more Egyptians working in official positions, Arabic had gradually replaced Turkish as the language of government. And laws against the slave trade freed thousands of slaves.

Egypt grew sugar and cotton, selling the products mostly to Britain, which was gaining an economic as well as military presence in Egypt. Meanwhile, some Egyptians began to talk of uniting the Nile Valley and the Nile Delta into an independent nation, free of foreign domination.

Cairo's pasha, Muhammad Ali *(facing page, bottom),* was an Albanian-born soldier of the Ottoman army. He embraced European technology and is shown negotiating with a British official *(facing page, top, seated on the bench).*

Two Cairos

During the 1800s, many Europeans came to Cairo as advisers. They lived in the European quarter west of Cairo's older neighborhoods. To provide more room for expansion, Lake Ezbekiya was filled in and built over.

European residents controlled industry, trade, and services in Cairo. They used the wealth they earned to build lavish athletic clubs, dance halls, and other recreational facilities. Europeans erected luxurious new houses, trying to copy the lifestyle they had enjoyed back home. Most Europeans' contact with native Cairenes was limited to talking with servants and tour guides.

Cairo's Egyptian population continued to live much as it had for centuries in the city's older, eastern section. Most people still dressed in traditional clothing, lived in simple homes with few furnishings, and traveled on horses, camels, and donkeys or by foot.

In contrast to educated Europeans, most Cairenes could not read or write. Most people were poor and could not afford to fix their crumbling homes and buildings. Neighborhoods became more and more crowded as people moved from the countryside to Cairo, hoping to find jobs in the growing city.

> *There are two Cairos, distinct in character, though but slenderly divided in site. There is a European Cairo, and there is an Egyptian Cairo.*
> —British historian Stanley Lane-Poole, 1902

As more and more Europeans moved to Cairo in the nineteenth century, European fashions and horse-drawn carriages became a common sight on city streets.

Cairo under the British

By 1880 Egypt was heavily in debt. The British had developed trade with Egypt, and a British company had purchased rights to the Suez Canal. When unrest in Cairo threatened the authority of the pasha in 1882, British troops occupied the city and took over Egypt's finances and government.

The growing European quarter along the Nile soon became the center of government and business. The palace at Ezbekiya where Napoleon had once lived became Shepheard's Hotel, the favorite place for European visitors to stay. Tourists came in droves to enjoy the mild Egyptian winter, visit ancient sites, and explore the exotic medieval city. A road suitable for carriages took visitors from Cairo to the Great Pyramid at Giza. The road crossed the Nile on a new permanent bridge that connected the outlying towns with the expanding city.

The British built new canals in the rural areas to improve irrigation. As a result, farmers grew more food and cotton. The

British also constructed a dam at Aswan, 400 miles to the south. The dam controlled the Nile's annual flooding. People stopped celebrating the rise of the river, although tourists continued to visit the Nilometer. Cairo's canals, which were no longer needed for water, were filled in. Some became streets for the increasing carriage traffic.

The British occupied Egypt through the first half of the twentieth century. They promised to eventually grant Egypt its independence. But even after they freed Egypt from Ottoman rule during World War I (1914–1918), the British retained control of most government positions.

As more and more Egyptians received educations in the new schools and universities, they became involved in managing their country's affairs. By the mid-1900s, Egyptian men and women worked in the government at all but the highest levels. Egyptians also served in all ranks of the military.

The stream of European tourists to Egypt included the French empress Eugénie *(facing page),* who visited in 1869 for the opening of the Suez Canal. Local Cairo residents mingle with Europeans in front of Shepheard's Hotel around 1928 *(above).*

The City Expands

Around the 1900s, Cairo's population began to increase. Deaths from disease fell because of improved health and sanitation. For example, the government required people to receive vaccinations against smallpox. A new sewer system helped reduce deaths from waste-borne diseases such as dysentery and cholera. But Cairo's population grew mainly because people from other parts of Egypt came to the city hoping to find work or better living conditions. Many of the newcomers were farmers or unskilled laborers who crowded into the older, poorer areas of the city.

Throughout the twentieth century, the city's population continued to grow quickly, especially after World War II (1939–1945). In response to the growing

Swank new apartment buildings rose in Cairo's older neighborhoods *(facing page)*. Tourists were amazed at the apartments' low rental rates. For example, in 1949, three-room apartments in the building at left rented for as little as 15 Egyptian pounds (about $60) per month.

population, new homes and apartment buildings were built on empty plots of land within the city limits. The city's borders expanded in all directions, especially to the north and northeast.

Several electric tram lines connected outlying neighborhoods to the city center. New bridges across the Nile made it possible for the city to expand onto large islands in the river and onto the river's west bank. Residences and shops lined the road leading to the pyramids at Giza. To the east, tens of thousands of people found living quarters in the tombs and mosques of the large Mamluk cemetery.

The city also grew upward. New high-rise buildings housed residential apartments as well as offices. Owners added new upper floors to old buildings. Landlords divided homes and apartments into smaller units, and extended families often shared their residences with each other.

Independence

British officials and troops ruled Egypt until 1952. In July, a military uprising freed Egypt from the rule of foreigners for the first time in more than two thousand years. Cairo became the capital of the new republic.

Gamal Abdel Nasser was elected president in 1956. New ways and old sometimes clashed as the new secular (non-religious) government made rapid social changes. Many of the new state's programs offended people who preferred traditional ways. These people still considered religious laws to be more important than government rules.

Nasser's reforms limited the amount of land a wealthy person could own. Banks, industries, and the Suez Canal came under Egyptian government control. Most Europeans left the city.

By the 1950s, many women were working outside the home, especially in jobs as government workers or teachers. In most cases, families needed women's salaries to get by. New laws gave women the right to vote, and new schools offered free education to everyone—adults as well as children. Secular universities opened, and classes at al-Azhar University were expanded to include medicine and other sciences. In spite of a rapid growth in

education, only about one in four Egyptians could read in the 1950s.

In the 1960s, a special settlement for Cairo's poor people was built on the rocky, dry land of the city's eastern hills. New health care and food programs helped improve the lives of needy families. The government worked to keep prices low for everyday products, including basic foods. In January 1977, Cairo's citizens rioted in the streets when the government announced rising prices for bread and other necessary foods. The protest was so strong that the government withdrew its plan.

An Egyptian tank patrols the streets of Cairo during the 1952 uprising *(left)*. President Gamal Abdel Nasser *(right)* greets enthusiastic crowds in 1956. During the 1977 food riots *(below)*, 34 people were killed and 409 injured.

Modern Cairo

In 1969 Cairo celebrated the one thousandth anniversary of the founding of the Fatimid city al-Qahira. Cairo remains Islamic, with Muslims making up more than 90 percent of its residents. The city is a center of Arabic culture and intellectual life. Al-Azhar University is still the foremost school of Islamic religious studies.

The original site of al-Qahira is a small part of a much larger metropolitan community. One in five Egyptians lives in the Cairo metropolitan area. With a high birth rate and a lower death rate due to modern advances in health care, Cairo continues to grow. Its population at the beginning of the twenty-first century is estimated to exceed 13 million.

Cairo's people are a mix of many ethnic groups. Some live modern lives, while others embrace traditional customs. They dress in American- or European-style clothes as well as in traditional robes. Women are veiled or unveiled as they choose. Some wear a modern veil that covers only the head or neck.

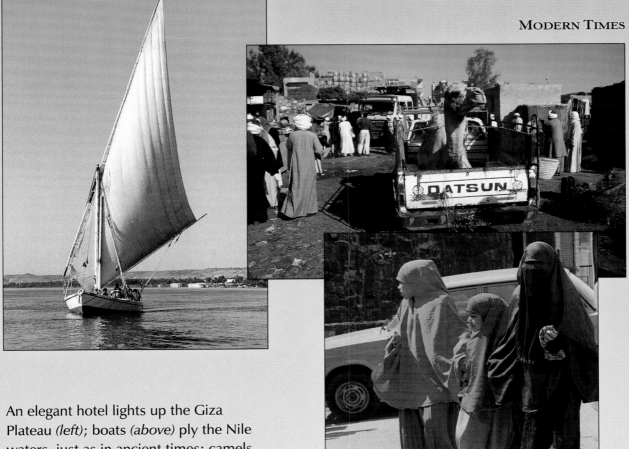

An elegant hotel lights up the Giza Plateau *(left)*; boats *(above)* ply the Nile waters, just as in ancient times; camels are bought and traded at market *(top right)*; and Cairo women go about their shopping in traditional dress *(right)*.

Historic mosques and other Islamic monuments reflect Cairo's fascinating history. The city has expanded to surround the remains of earlier times, such as Giza's pyramids, the ancient obelisk (stone column) in the northern suburb of Heliopolis, and the Coptic churches of Old Cairo. More than five thousand years of Cairene history are on display in the city's many museums.

Tourists from all over the world arrive at Cairo's modern airport, stay in high-rise hotels, and walk along the Corniche (the broad street that fronts the Nile River). They shop in the city's modern department stores or in the medieval markets of the Khan el-Khalili. Modern Cairo faces the challenges of feeding, housing, educating, and providing jobs for its fast-growing population. In addition, its citizens are looking for ways to adopt new technologies while still maintaining older, valued Islamic traditions. Cairo is a complex society with many different strains of culture. It remains a fascinating crossroads of the world.

Cairo Timeline

	First Millennium B.C.	First and Second Millennium A.D.

3000 B.C.–A.D. 971
Pre-Cairo Settlements and the Founding of Cairo

3000 B.C.	Ancient Egypt established with Memphis as the capital
2550 B.C.	Great Pyramid built
525 B.C.	Persians conquer Egypt; Nile–Red Sea canal opens
332 B.C.	Greeks, under Alexander the Great, conquer Egypt
30 B.C.	Romans conquer Egypt

A.D. 45	Christianity introduced to Egypt
A.D. 284	Coptic calendar begins
A.D. 395	Egypt becomes part of Byzantine Empire
A.D. 640	Arabs, led by Am'r, invade Egypt; al-Fustat established; Nile–Red Sea canal reopened
A.D. 750	Islamic Abbasids conquer Egypt; palace city of Medinat al-Askar founded north of al-Fustat
A.D. 870	Ibn Tulun establishes independent dynasty of Tulunids in Egypt; palace city of al-Qatai built north of al-Fustat
A.D. 969	Al-Qahira (Cairo) founded by Fatimid Dynasty; Shia Islam introduced
A.D. 971	Al-Azhar Mosque founded

A.D. 971–1250
Early Cairo

A.D. 1168	Fatimid overlords burn al-Fustat; Saladin arrives in Egypt
A.D. 1169	Saladin becomes sultan of Egypt under Fatimids
A.D. 1171	Saladin becomes sultan of Abbasid Dynasty; Sunni Islam restored to Egypt; Citadel built and Cairo's walls extended

A.D. 1250–1517
Cairo under Mamluk Rule

A.D. 1249	Queen Shajrat al-Durr assumes power
A.D. 1250	Mamluks take control of Cairo
A.D. 1348	Plague kills 200,000 Cairo residents
A.D. 1382	Circassian Mamluks take control; Khan el-Khalili founded
A.D. 1498	Portuguese navigator Vasco da Gama reaches India by sailing around Africa, opening Southeast Asian trade to Europe and ending Cairo's control of the spice trade

Second Millennium A.D.

A.D. 1517–1798 **Cairo under the** **Ottoman Turks**	**A.D. 1517**	Ottoman Turks conquer Egypt; Ottoman pasha installed in Cairo
A.D. 1798–1952 **Western European** **Influence and** **Nationalism**	**A.D. 1798**	Napoleon invades Egypt and takes over Cairo
	A.D. 1801	French troops leave Egypt under combined Turkish-British threat
	A.D. 1805	Muhammad Ali becomes pasha of Egypt
	A.D. 1811	Muhammad Ali massacres Mamluk chiefs, ending Mamluk influence
	A.D. 1863	Ismail becomes ruler
	A.D. 1869	Suez Canal opens
	A.D. 1882	British troops occupy Cairo; British officials take over government; a British company takes over Suez Canal
	A.D. 1902	British build dam at Aswan
	A.D. 1922	Under British control, Egypt becomes constitutional monarchy
A.D. 1952– **Modern Times**	**A.D. 1952**	Military uprising leads to Egyptian independence
	A.D. 1956	Last British troops leave Egypt; Gamal Abdel Nasser becomes president; Nasser nationalizes Suez Canal and proclaims new constitution; women receive right to vote
	A.D. 1969	Millennial anniversary of Cairo's founding
	A.D. 1970	Aswan High Dam completed
	A.D. 1986	Cairo reaches size of more than 80 square miles and population of 9.7 million
	A.D. 1994	Cairo hosts the United Nations International Conference on Population and Development

Books about Egypt and Cairo

Corrick, James. *The Byzantine Empire*. San Diego: Lucent Books, 1996.

Day, Nancy. *Your Travel Guide to Ancient Egypt*. Minneapolis: Runestone Press, 2001.

Egypt in Pictures. Minneapolis: Lerner Publications Company, 1992.

Harris, Geraldine. *Cultural Atlas for Young People: Ancient Egypt*. New York: Facts on File, 1990.

Kenneth, Frances, and Caroline MacDonald-Haig. *Ethnic Dress*. New York: Facts on File, 1997.

Knight, Khadijah. *Islam* (World Religions Series). Austin, Texas: Raintree/Steck-Vaughn, 1995.

Macaulay, David. *Pyramid*. New York: Houghton Mifflin, 1982.

Pitkänen, Matti A., with Reijo Härkönen. *The Children of Egypt*. Minneapolis: Carolrhoda Books, Inc., 1991.

Streissguth, Tom. *Egypt*. (Globe-trotters Club series). Minneapolis: Carolrhoda Books, Inc., 1999.

Index

About the Author and Illustrator

Joan D. Barghusen worked for many years as director of museum education at the Oriental Institute of the University of Chicago. Her interest in ancient Mediterranean civilizations has taken her to Egypt, Tunisia, and Malta. In addition to several books, her publications include articles on archaeology and history in *Cricket* and *Calliope* magazines. She lives in Chicago, Illinois.

Bob Moulder of Derby, England, studied art in Belfast, Northern Ireland. He is a specialist in historical artwork and comic strips. His artwork has appeared in leading publications in the United Kingdom. He works with the Oxford Illustrators and Designers Group in Oxford, England.

Acknowledgments

For quoted material: Susan Jane Staffa. *Conquest and Fusion: The Social Evolution of Cairo A.D. 642–1850.* (Leiden: E. J. Brill, 1977), pp. 10, 22; William Popper. *History of Egypt 1382–1469 A.D. Part III, 1412–1422 A.D.* (Berkeley: U. of California Press, 1957), p. 19; Desmond Stewart. *Cairo 5500 Years.* (New York: Thomas Y. Crowell Co., 1968), p. 20; Avner Gil'adi. *Children of Islam: Concepts of Childhood in Medieval Muslim Society.* (New York: St. Martin's Press, 1992), p. 28; Boaz Shoshan. *Popular Culture in Medieval Cairo.* (Cambridge U.P., 1993), pp. 30, 32; Husain Haddawy. *The Arabian Nights.* (New York: W. W. Norton & Co., 1990), p. 34; Charles Issawi. *An Arab Philosophy of History.* (London: John Murray, 1950), p. 37; Michael W. Dols. *The Black Death in the Middle East.* (Princeton U. P., 1977), p. 39; Janet L. Abu-Lughod. *Cairo: 1001 Years of the City Victorious.* (Princeton U. P., 1971), pp. 40, 45; S. Moreh. *Al-Jabarti's Chronicle of the First Seven Months of the French Occupation of Egypt.* (Leiden: E. J. Brill, 1975), p. 47; Edward William Lane. *An Account of the Manners and Customs of the Modern Egyptians.* (New York: Dover Publications, Inc., 1973), p. 48; Stanley Lane-Poole. *The Story of Cairo.* (London: J. M. Dent & Co., 1902), p. 50.

For photos and fine-art reproductions: Bridgeman Art Library, pp. 4 (top) (view of the city, from the Citadel (photo) Cairo, Egypt), 18–19 (*The Subsiding of the Nile*, 1873 by Frederick Goodall, Russell-Cotes Art Gallery and Museum, Bournemouth, UK), 21 (30359 f.86 *Saladin, Sultan of Egypt and Syria* from the "Six Ages of the World" represented by historical personalities from Adam to Pope Boniface VIII, Italian, 15th century/British Library, London, UK), 23 (*A Mameluke Exercising,* 1802, published by R. Bowyer, Bonhams, London, UK), 29 (*Interior of a School, Cairo,* 1890, by John Frederick Lewis, Victoria & Albert Museum, London, UK), 32 (*The Street and Mosque of the Ghooreyah, Cairo,* by John Frederick Lewis, The Fine Art Society, London, UK), 34 (bottom) (*A Sunday in Cairo,* 1884, by Charles Wilda, The Fine Art Society, London, UK), 40 (top) (*A Janissary and a Merchant in Cairo,* illustration from 'The Valley of the Nile,' engraved by Charles Bour (1814–81) pub. by Lemercier, 1848 (litho) by Emile Prisse (1807–79) (after)/Stapleton Collection, UK), 43 (*Street Scene, Cairo,* by Charles Theodore Frere (Bey), Whitford & Hughes, London, UK), 47 (*The Revolt at Cairo, 1798,* 1810, by Anne Louis Girodet-Trioson, Château de Versailles, France/Peter Willi); © Carl E. Kotapish, pp. 4 (bottom), 59 (left); Art Resource, NY, pp. 8, 9, 26 (Victoria & Albert Museum, London, Great Britain), 27 (National Library, Cairo, Egypt, Giraudon), 40 (bottom) (© Erich Lessing); The Granger Collection, pp. 13, 45 (central and inset), 48 (bottom); SuperStock, pp. 20, 54; Christie's Images/SuperStock, pp. 34 (top), 42, 52; North Wind Picture Archives, pp. 37, 51; Christie's Images, p. 46; Mary Evans, p. 48 (top); Liaison, pp. 53, 56; AP/Wide World, pp. 55, 57 (bottom), 59 (bottom right); Corbis/Bettmann-UPI, p. 57 (top); ©Will and Deni McIntyre/Stone, p. 58; © Liba Taylor/Panos Pictures, p. 59 (upper right). Cover: SuperStock.